Original title:
Tales from the Tall Trees

Copyright © 2025 Creative Arts Management OÜ
All rights reserved.

Author: Natalia Harrington
ISBN HARDBACK: 978-1-80567-441-2
ISBN PAPERBACK: 978-1-80567-740-6

Secrets Swaying in the Breeze

In the branches, whispers laugh,
Squirrels gossip of their craft.
A crow caws, thinks he's a star,
But he's just a bird from afar.

Journey Through the Timbered Shadows

Adventures hide between the boughs,
Where raccoons dance and no one bows.
They steal the snacks we thought we'd keep,
While nature fuels their nighttime leap.

Reverie of the Wandering Deer

A deer in specs, looking for a pal,
Accidentally startled by a gal.
With a wiggle and a fluffy tail,
He trots away, leaving a trail.

Chasing Light in the Leafy Treetops

A light beam tumbles, the critters chase,
Each furry face filled with silly grace.
They leap and bound, try to take flight,
While laughing leaves join in the light.

The Symphony of the Shaded Grove

In the grove where shadows play,
Squirrels dance the night away,
A raccoon conducts the spark,
To the rhythm of a lark.

The owls hoot a jazzy tune,
While fireflies light up the moon,
The branches sway in happy glee,
Nature's own cacophony.

Woodpeckers tap in perfect beat,
With frogs croaking, oh so sweet,
The trees all sway, a bobbing crew,
Who knew they had rhythm too?

As branches bend and leaves take flight,
The symphony fades with the night,
Yet every critter, bold and small,
Leaves the grove, feeling ten feet tall.

The Hidden Heart of the Forest

In the woods where secrets lie,
A bear in jammies hears a sigh,
The trees gossip about the sun,
And oaky puns are such good fun.

A rabbit puts on a silly hat,
While the fox tries to chase a cat,
They trip over roots, laugh, and roll,
As the trees chuckle from their pole.

Mushrooms sprout with grinning grace,
Poking fun at the snail's slow pace,
Trees whisper jokes in the breeze,
While the flowers sway with ease.

In this forest, delight is found,
Where every creature spins around,
With laughter echoing all day long,
The heart of this place sings a funny song.

Lessons from the Lush Canopy

In a forest where squirrels play,
Acorns fly their own way.
A chipmunk stows some snacks away,
While a crow mocks their ballet.

Rabbits hop and squirrels tease,
As shadows dance with playful ease.
A raccoon tiptoes, oh so sly,
As laughter echoes from the sky.

The trees whisper secrets bold,
Of mischief that never gets old.
Leaves chuckle at the clumsy stag,
While the shy deer just snorts and wag.

With every rustle, joy does bloom,
In a world where fun finds room.
Where branches sway and giggles blend,
Even the grumpy fox finds a friend.

The Poetry of Green Gentle Giants

Tall giants sway with every breeze,
With limbs that tickle and tease.
They sway and bend in afternoon light,
Always ready for a playful fight.

Branches stretch, a great display,
As the critters come out to play.
A blue jay pirouettes on a limb,
While a rabbit shows off on a whim.

Leaves sing songs with rustling lines,
Breezes share bits of punchy pines.
Their laughter rings through the bright green,
The funniest show you've ever seen.

In the shade, a soft breeze flows,
Giggling trees – oh how it shows!
With gentle giants, joy abounds,
In this green world where fun resounds.

Memory Lingers in the Leaves

As fall approaches, leaves giggle soft,
Each one sways, taking flight aloft.
Whispers of colors bright and bold,
Funny tales of old are retold.

A maple knows it once wore red,
While birch recalls the ants it fed.
In every rustle, a secret shared,
Of young hearts laughed and grown unprepared.

Wind carries chuckles that gently soar,
Tickling branches, forever more.
The past swings in a playful cheer,
As the future dances, drawing near.

In the embrace of golden skies,
The trees giggle with knowing eyes.
Memories held in every shade,
In the laughter of leaves, fun's portrayed.

The Secrets Carried by the Wind

The wind whistles tunes, a witty jest,
Whipping through branches, teasing the best.
It flirts with the flowers, so carefree,
Sharing words of whimsy, full of glee.

A leaf catches a ride, spinning around,
Telling jokes that can leave you unbound.
The whispers flow with each crooked bend,
In the arms of the breeze, all troubles suspend.

With elation, it swirls near the brook,
Where turtles glide as if they're in a book.
Each ripple giggles, a sweet serenade,
As secrets unravel, the fun won't fade.

So when the wind sings and plays its part,
Listen closely, it speaks to the heart.
In this realm where laughter twirls and spins,
The secrets carried delight and grins.

Whispers Among the Canopy

Squirrel wears spectacles, how absurd,
He reads the fine print on each bird.
A raccoon in a top hat, quite the sight,
Juggling acorns under the moonlight.

A parrot named Polly sings off key,
Mocking the wind with a loud honoree.
In the branches, laughter fills the air,
As the trees gossip without a care.

Chipmunks complain of the nutty plight,
While owls chuckle at their own insight.
The breeze tickles branches, starts a cheer,
Nature's own stand-up in the open sphere.

Oh listen close to the rustling leaves,
For comedy hops where the sunlight weaves.
In this green theater where laughter reigns,
Beneath the canopy, joy never wanes.

Secrets of the Wooded Heights

In the heights where the owls delight,
The trees have secrets that come to light.
A wise old elm whispers quite sly,
"Did you hear that? The dandelions fly!"

A beaver plays tricks with a wink and a splash,
While hedgehogs giggle in a bushy mash.
The sunbeams play tag on the forest floor,
And the mushrooms plot mischief — oh, what a score!

A chipmunk debates with a wise old crow,
On whether the clouds will come, or just go.
They argue and jest as the shadows grow,
In the wooded heights where the laughter flows.

Every creature conspires, they can't be wrong,
In this quirky corner, everyone belongs.
It's a comedy club where the jokes are bright,
Unveiling secrets through the day and night.

The Dance of the Leafy Giants

Tall trees sway with a graceful cheer,
Their branches open wide, come take a peer.
Beneath their skirts, the squirrels spin,
In a ballet of life, let the fun begin!

A fox in a tutu twirls with flair,
While frogs in shades bask without a care.
The roots tap along to a murky beat,
Turning the woods into a dance floor sweet.

When the wind plays music, they bust a groove,
With acorns as maracas, they start to move.
It's a jolly jamboree, they can't resist,
In the realm of the giants, laughter persists.

Every leaf has a story, every trunk a joke,
As the sun dips low, the forest awoke.
In this leafy bal room, they twist and twine,
Nature's own party, sublime and divine.

Echoes Beneath the Boughs

Beneath the boughs, where echoes are free,
A chorus of critters sings joyfully.
The badgers tell tales of a night well spent,
While the bunnies hop along, all cheerful and bent.

A frog croaks out puns to a curious deer,
"Why did the chicken? Oh, let me be clear!"
Laughter ricochets off each tree trunk wide,
As chipmunks chuckle and squirrels confide.

The shadows grow longer, the sun starts to fade,
Yet the giggles of critters refuse to be laid.
Every rustle and whisper has humor inside,
In the echoing forest, where laughter won't hide.

Dance to the sound of their merry embrace,
In a tangled world of whimsical grace.
The woods come alive with a raucous cheer,
And beneath the boughs, there's plenty to hear.

Chronicles Written in Chlorophyll

In the canopy where squirrels dance,
Mice throw parties, they take a chance.
With nuts for snacks and leaves for hats,
They groove to the tunes of chatty cats.

A parrot juggles acorns with flair,
While a raccoon claims he's a millionaire.
Chasing shadows, they leap and twirl,
In their leafy world, life's a whirl!

Oh, the pine trees giggle, their bark so rough,
As chipmunks boast, "We're just too tough!"
A deer rolls eyes, "Is this a dream?"
Nature's jesters, the ultimate team!

Each bark tells a story, each rustle a laugh,
The woodland's heart is a quirky half.
With every breeze, secrets unfurl,
In the grand old woods, it's a silly world!

Forest Fairytales: A Natural History

Underneath mushrooms, tales come to life,
Frogs in top hats, avoiding the strife.
Snakes tell jokes in a whispering hiss,
While owls eye-roll, "You must be remiss."

Wandering brook sings a bubble-verse,
Through comical grasses, oh, how they immerse!
Elks wear glasses, claiming they're wise,
While the wise old fox just spins his lies.

The breeze carries laughter from leaf to leaf,
Each rustling branch a punchline — relief!
A squirrel quips, "This acorn's a prize!"
Boasting of treasure, in a world so wise.

In the twilight's glow, the shadows play tricks,
Whispers of laughter, a forest mix.
With twinkling stars, the night seems to cheer,
In this green wonderland, joy's always near!

Dialogues of the Stars and Spruce

Stars gossip softly with the tall, green trees,
"Have you heard about Luna, sailing the breeze?"
The spruces respond, "Oh, she's quite the sight,
Wearing her gown spun from pure moonlight!"

Branches sway gently, tickled by starlight,
While crickets chirp in the cool of the night.
"Who's the comedian?" asks one bold fir,
"Is it the owl or the bright firefly stir?"

The siloed maples join in with sass,
"I've got a pun from the moment folks pass!"
With echoes of laughter, a treetop glee,
When tall tales rise from roots to the lea.

Overhead, the sky paints mischief and fun,
Surrounded by wonders, all hopping and run!
From the height of the boughs to the depth of the earth,
Laughter enchanted, of nature's great birth!

The Spirit of the Swaying Timbers

In the woods, where shadows play hide and seek,
Timbers sway, chatting, with branches unique.
"Did you hear what the willow said?"
"Something about a dream of being wed!"

With twinkling laughter, the birch joins in,
"Finding a partner is quite the win!"
Acorns tumble, creating a sound,
As giggles emerge from the soft, leafy ground.

The tall maples boast, "We swayed for a while,
Receiving compliments, we planted a smile!"
While the oaks with dignity nod and reply,
"Being majestic isn't just to comply."

With breezes that tickle, they dance with flair,
Under the starlight, without a care.
A forest of laughter, secrets entwined,
In the spirit of woods, joy you will find!

Nature's Canvas in the Upper Reaches

In the branches, squirrels conspire,
Plotting mischief, never tire.
With acorns scattered, they do play,
Nuts and giggles rule the day.

Birds in top hats, a fancy flight,
Waltzing on air, oh what a sight!
With feathers bright, they strut and preen,
A feathered ball for all to glean.

Sunshine giggles through the green,
Playing hide and seek, unseen.
Leaves chuckle softly, rustled glee,
Nature's canvas, wild and free.

Underneath the leafy shade,
A raccoon juggles, unafraid.
With berries tossed into the fray,
A laugh parade, hip-hip-hooray!

Whispers Through the Width

In the trees, a gossip spree,
Branches sway with wild decree.
"Did you see that silly crow?"
"Wearing socks! Oh, what a show!"

Breezes chat in breezy tones,
A fox pipes up, with playful moans.
"Have you heard the latest tweet?"
"I think it's all about the beat!"

Frogs croak puns, on lily pads,
Their laughter echoing, never sads.
Fireflies flicker, jokes alight,
Illuminating the starry night.

Every leaf a chuckle shared,
In the woods, no one is scared.
The trees are ticklish, swaying bliss,
Underneath this green abyss.

Echoes Beneath the Boughs

A family of rabbits hops around,
Their silly antics, quite profound.
One bounces high, then lands with style,
Creating socks with flair, and a smile.

Owls are hooting jokes at night,
With raucous laughter, such delight.
"Why did the bat fly up so high?"
"To see his friends, up in the sky!"

Under the boughs, shadows play,
Tree trunks dodge and twist away.
Old oak tells tales, not too wise,
With creaks and groans, what a surprise!

Echoes of chuckles softly ring,
Through the greens, the joy they bring.
Here in the woods, where fun admires,
Life is brighter, fueled by choirs.

Harmony Among the High Branches

In the high branches, monkeys swing,
   Tails entwined, oh what a fling!
  They toss around bananas bright,
   And giggle with all their might.

Parrots squawk, a raucous tune,
Singing loudly, morning to noon.
"That's not a branch, it's my new house!"
  "Careful there, you silly louse!"

The breeze brings whispers of delight,
  As crickets chirp into the night.
  A dance-off starts under the moon,
  With twirls and flips, they all attune.

Nature's orchestra, play it loud,
With every rustle, we feel proud.
Among the trees, life's merry spin,
  A joyful jamboree begins!

Memories of the Majestic Oaks

Once I saw a squirrel run,
He tripped and landed on a bun.
Those acorns flew, oh what a sight!
The oak just laughed with pure delight.

The bark once told a silly joke,
About a wise old leaf and smoke.
They giggled till the sun dipped low,
Then danced around in shadows' glow.

Once a branch wore a wizard's hat,
Claimed he could turn a cat to gnat.
But when he waved, it changed to pie,
And all the birds began to fly.

Underneath the oak's wide arm,
Squirrels whispered tales of charm.
With every gust, they'd sway and tease,
While rustling leaves sang with the breeze.

The Secret Life of Gnarled Roots

Beneath the soil, a party grew,
With worms and bugs, a wiggly crew.
They giggled while they danced all night,
In the dark, they found their light.

One root wore a disco ball,
Bouncing rhythms for one and all.
The earthworms twirled, the beetles pranced,
And even mushrooms joined the dance.

They chatted about the trees above,
And how the shade was their sweet love.
With mud pies served in cups of rain,
The underground was never plain.

When morning came, the roots grew tired,
Their silly games now all expired.
But whispered laughs still float around,
In tales of fun just underground.

Ballads of the Branching Paths

A branch once took a funny quest,
To seek out nuts and find the best.
He wandered far, got lost in thought,
And found a hat that someone bought.

With hats piled high, he'd strut and preen,
A fashionista of the green.
But when the wind swirled 'round so quick,
He lost his hat—oh what a trick!

The birds all chirped, "What a disgrace!
A tree in fashion can't keep pace!"
So sideways grew that clever twig,
In style and boughs, he did a jig.

Now every path holds such a tale,
Of branches bold that never fail.
For in the woods, it's hard to know,
Which trail to take and where to go.

The Voice of the Old Growth

An ancient tree with wisdom vast,
Spoke tales of ages long since passed.
"I once saw birds in funny hats,
And squirrels trying to juggle mats!"

With creaky voice, he shared a grin,
Of how the sun would come and spin.
The leaves all laughed as winds took flight,
Their rustling joy a pure delight.

The moss replied with rhymes so sweet,
Of dancing shadows at his feet.
"Let's gather round and sing all day,
While branches sway and branches play!"

So under skies of blue and gray,
The old tree beckoned all to stay.
In laughter, wisdom intertwined,
In every rustle, joy you'd find.

Enchanted Glades and Starlit Paths

In a glade where fairies rest,
A squirrel wore a tiny vest.
He danced around with gleeful chirps,
While rabbits giggled, doing flips.

The owls wore glasses, reading lore,
While wise old foxes shared some more.
A hedgehog baked a berry pie,
Claiming it would help them fly.

Under starlit skies, they pranced,
With moonbeams shining, all entranced.
The raccoons played a game of tag,
As everyone in laughter wagged.

With laughter ringing through the night,
The trees swayed softly, pure delight.
In the forest's whimsical embrace,
They found the fun in every space.

The Storyteller's Roots

Beneath the roots where stories flow,
A gnome recites from long ago.
His voice is loud, his hat is tall,
As creatures gather, big and small.

A fox with a top hat tells his joke,
His punchline makes the badger choke.
The bunny snickers, two front teeth,
While weaving tales beneath the wreath.

A turtle claims he's seen the moon,
But whispers 'twas a scavenger's tune.
The trees all chuckle, leaves a-quake,
As mushrooms pop up, oh what a break!

In this nook where stories blend,
Laughter's the language without end.
They bask in memories, old and new,
While magic dances in the view.

Beneath the Emerald Veil

Underneath the emerald shade,
A chameleon starts a parade.
With flashes bright and colors bold,
He tricks the trees, or so I'm told.

A bear in bow ties struts around,
While singing songs without a sound.
The pine trees sway, their branches blend,
As squirrels cheer for their fuzzy friend.

The wind whispers secrets, oh so sly,
While ants form conga lines nearby.
A playful lizard sets the beat,
As crickets play on tiny feet.

Beneath the stars, their shadows play,
In laughter's arms, they spend the day.
The forest's life, a lively spree,
Where fun's the rule, and wild, carefree.

Conversations of the Evergreen Giants

The towering trees began to sway,
Discussing life in their own way.
One trunk shared tales of ticklish moss,
While branches giggled, laughing across.

A squirrel piped in with a hasty blurt,
Saying ants had held a fancy shirt.
The oaks just chuckled, all in glee,
Knowing trunks don't wear clothes, you see!

A pine tree fretted over the breeze,
Worried that it might shake his leaves.
But the others laughed, not a care,
For trees just dance, swaying with flair.

As the stars peeked in with a grin,
The giants laughed, letting joy win.
In evergreen conversations, bright,
The forest thrived in sheer delight.

Comrades of the Canopy

In the treetops high they play,
Squirrels gossip all day.
Parrots squawk with glee and flair,
While owls just sit and stare.

Branches creak, the leaves all shake,
A dance of limbs, it's no mistake.
The raccoons laugh, the woodpecker taps,
As creatures join in funny mishaps.

Up there the world looks quite absurd,
With every twist and silly word.
They leap and bound, they swing and sway,
Living life in a comical way.

Friendships formed in bark and leaf,
A canopy's joy, beyond belief.
With every rustle, a new delight,
In the branches, everything's bright!

The Dance of the Swaying Doughs

The branches bob like dancers free,
With trees that sway in harmony.
A gust of wind brings a hearty cheer,
As leaves turn round with a twist and a leer.

The squirrels join in pirouettes,
Finding acorns, making bets.
While chipmunks cheer and root them on,
In this leafy, breezy con.

A raccoon in a top hat prances,
Even he can't resist the chances.
With all the laughter in the air,
It seems trees love a wild affair!

The tree trunks twist and bend with grace,
As laughter echoes through the space.
With leafy laughter, trees ignite,
A whimsical show in the moonlight!

Stories Carved in Knotted Grain

Beneath the bark, old secrets dwell,
In curls and swirls, they laugh and tell.
The raccoon reads each engraved line,
What once was sad, now is divine.

Knots and twists create a tale,
Of trees that danced without fail.
A squirrel giggles at a time gone by,
As beetles swarm and butterflies fly.

The woodpeckers tap with rhythmic flair,
In the grains, they find stories rare.
Each peck is a punchline, a quirk, a jest,
From the whispers of wood, they never rest.

Laughter rings out with every groove,
The stories alive, they burst and move.
In knotted grain, friendships intertwine,
A comical forest, divine by design!

The Whispering Woods' Heritage

Through whispers of leaves, the stories flow,
Echoes of laughter in breezes that blow.
The trees giggle as they spread their cheer,
Sharing funny moments, year after year.

The foxes cling to trunks, hanging tight,
As they watch owls take off in flight.
Rustling roots, a secret surprise,
Shapes in the shadows, oh how they rise!

With every branch, a chuckle so near,
In the whispering woods, there's nothing to fear.
Tales of mischief and friendly feuds,
In the laughter of nature, everyone's wooed.

Lively echoes twirl round and round,
In this merry land where joy is found.
With whispers soft and spirits that fly,
The woods contain joy that never runs dry!

Songs of the Wind-Flecked Canopy

A squirrel sang a cheeky tune,
Between the leaves and bright balloon.
The crow joined in with cawing glee,
As branches twirled in wild jubilee.

The acorns fell with little plops,
As critters danced, there were no stops.
An owl who hooted, all wise and round,
Was laughed at by a mouse he found.

A breeze blew through, and leaves would sway,
Mistaken for a prankster's play.
The shadows flicked with mischief's spark,
As creatures plotted 'til it was dark.

In laughter high, the forest spry,
Each secret shade and twinkling eye.
In every nook, a giggle spun,
Where sunlight flickers, joy begun.

Roots Deep, Branches High

Roots clung tightly, all dressed in mud,
While branches stretched and made a thud.
The earthbugs laughed at the tree's great height,
And dared the leaves to join the flight.

The winds would whisper, 'Oh dear grass!
You're just too short to give us sass.'
But grass just shrugged, 'I dance my way,
While you stand still, in dreams you lay.'

Beetles boasted of shiny shells,
While ants marched boldly under spells.
Each trunk recounted ancient lore,
As snickers echoed evermore.

'Roots deep, branches high,' proclaimed the sky,
While mountains giggled, asking why.
Together they shared the grandest show,
In this company of friendlies, row by row.

The Kisses of Dappled Sunlight

Sunlight danced on leaves above,
Kissing the ground with warmth and love.
The shadows played a silly game,
While light and dark competed for fame.

A shy little rabbit hid and peered,
From patches where sunbeams reared.
It hopped out quick, then back to hide,
As laughter echoed, far and wide.

The light would tickle all in sight,
While laughter sparked the leafy height.
The woodland creatures joined with cheer,
Creating joy that echoed near.

In dappled patches, fun would follow,
For every beam would gleam and hollow.
The sun's bright kisses filled the air,
With every giggle, every dare.

Guardians of the Green Retreat

In woods so grand, the guardians play,
With leafy crowns, they rule the day.
A twirling fox, with leaps so bold,
Conducts the choir with stories told.

The bushes rustle, secrets shared,
As laughter bursts, the forest fared.
The guardians wink with every swing,
While acorns drop like gifts from spring.

The birds, in chorus, sang their tune,
In harmony with the soft monsoons.
A turtle tripped, while running free,
And tumbled down, to join the spree.

In cozy knots, the friends unite,
As moonlight kisses the verdant sight.
For in this haven, joy takes flight,
With every giggle, day and night.

Mysteries Amidst Moss and Leaves

In shadows deep where squirrels stare,
The acorns dance, a wild affair.
A raccoon dons a hat too small,
Deciding whether to play ball.

The whispers of the bark so wise,
Tell tales of pranks beneath the skies.
A snail slips by, a slippery chap,
Wonders if he's missed the map.

A fox courts a spider, quite droll,
While fireflies flicker—a dance, a stroll.
They giggle together, each silly game,
As trees roll their eyes at the same old fame.

In this green world where stories sprout,
Laughter weaves 'round without a doubt.
Mossy carpets soften every fall,
As creatures unite for a comical ball.

Legends from the Lush Expanse

Among the leaves where whispers hide,
A turtle chuckles, oh what a ride!
He tells of a deer with legs like spaghetti,
Who tripped on roots and fell quite petty.

The owls spin yarns of a party gone wrong,
With frogs singing off-key, oh so strong!
A jam session breaks at the break of dawn,
With crickets joining in, a marvelous con.

Beneath the ferns, a badger's bold,
He dances in moonlight, not quite controlled.
His friends can't believe the sight so rare,
As laughter erupts, they dance without care.

In the lush expanse where mischief thrives,
The creatures unite, and joy arrives.
Each giggle and snicker, a leaf on the breeze,
Crafts legends anew with delightful ease.

The Silent Watchers Above

High in the branches, old stories dangle,
With woodpeckers tapping, it's quite the jangle.
A squirrel with acorns, plotting a heist,
While owls guard secrets, precise and sliced.

The wind whispers jokes that drift ever near,
As tree trunks chuckle, their bark full of cheer.
Beneath waving branches, shadows do play,
Inviting wise critters for a raucous day.

A parrot squawks, "What's green and can't fly?"
The answer escapes with a giggle nearby.
The canopy watches, eyes twinkling with glee,
As antics unfold, wild and carefree.

In a world up high where laughter will burst,
The watchers are silent, their stories unrehearsed.
Every rustle and shake brings smiles anew,
As the forest responds with a playful view.

Dreams Hidden in the Grove

In the heart of the grove, where silence is loud,
A hedgehog dreams of a circus crowd.
With juggling beetles and ants on parade,
The night's magic sits as that vision is made.

The trees sway gently, roots deep in cheer,
Whispering dreams of the critters near.
A chubby raccoon claims the king's throne,
Pretending the moon is his shimmering bone.

The butterflies giggle, tickling the air,
As the tiny grass dancers perform without care.
A fox in a tutu twirls to the beat,
While the stars overhead tap their feet.

With each nightfall, the grove's tales grow,
Planted in laughter, a wild ebb and flow.
So, come join the fun as dreams take their flight,
In the secret of shadows, we dance 'til the night.

Mystique of the Woodland Threshold

Beneath the leafy boughs, critters plot,
A raccoon wearing shades, oh what a thought!
Squirrels chase acorns with acrobatic flair,
While the wise old owl just sits in his chair.

Mushrooms gossip, 'Did you see that show?'
A twist of fate when the fox played the piano.
A squirrel in a cape, dancing with grace,
Leaves giggle and wiggle, a woodland embrace.

Hiding behind the pines, a hedgehog laughs,
Trying to juggle his tiny wooden staffs.
With laughter ringing clear, the forest hums,
As laughter and mischief in the daylight comes.

Whispers among the branches shout out loud,
The woodpecker claims, "I'm the best in the crowd!"
Everyone joins in, what a silly spree,
In this quirky world, oh, what fun to be free!

Timber Tales Forgotten

Once a squirrel with a coat all too bright,
Thought he'd impress the trees with his height.
He climbed and he stumbled, he tumbled down fast,
Now he's the punchline of jokes from the past.

The wise old tortoise, with wisdom to share,
Spins tales of a rabbit who just didn't care.
He ran for the prize, but tripped on a root,
Now he tells tales of his own clumsy loot.

Old logs whisper softly, their stories go slow,
Of a snail who raced, but forgot where to go.
He'd tell you his secret, if only he could,
The race isn't worth it when you're stuck in the wood.

In the glade, rabbits play tag with delight,
Chasing their shadows as day turns to night.
As owls hoot a tune, and the stars start to gleam,
The forest is alive with a whimsical dream!

The Grace of the Aged Bark

Old bark stands proudly, a storyteller's friend,
Sharing wild secrets that twist and extend.
A gopher with glasses adjusts his big specs,
As he learns of the woods from the wise, knotty hex.

Sprightly young saplings lean close for a listen,
While the branches above sway, as though they're on a mission.
A squirrel rolls past, in a whirlwind of fun,
Chasing shadows that flicker in the golden sun.

The badger, quite grumpy, demands a soft seat,
But a family of ants claims it's their favorite treat.
With a sigh and a huff, he mutters his plight,
While the woodpecker chuckles, "Just stay out of sight!"

Raccoons dance crazy, making sparks fly,
While the fireflies flutter, as the moon starts to sigh.
In this grand old forest, what a riotous lark,
It's the grace of the aged, waving trees with a spark!

Ancient Voices in the Foliage

The trees hold a chorus of giggles and cheers,
As fern fronds whisper through laughter and tears.
A raccoon with a cape, claims he's a knight,
In search of lost treasures hidden from sight.

A mouse with a hat, croons a silly song,
About a cow that jumped over a twig all along.
With a hop and a skip, she takes to the air,
But lands in a puddle—mozzarella beware!

Beneath the wise branches, old stories collide,
Of cousins and critters who far too often slide.
The pine cones roll out, sharing secrets galore,
While the hedgehogs all giggle, they tumble and snore.

In this jolly green realm, where dreams intertwine,
Laughter lingers long over berries and wine.
So gather, dear friends, let mirth weave its spell,
In ancient foliage, where all is quite well!

Dialogues in the Leafy Realm

In the branches, whispers loud,
Squirrels gossip, gather a crowd.
"Did you see that cat?" one chimes,
"Oh please, we've had worse times!"

The parrot squawks, a snicker shared,
"Last week, my nest got impaired!
A raccoon failed at his grand heist,
His stolen loot? Just a moldy slice!"

Before the owl can hoot his view,
The frogs croak, "That's old news too!"
The wise old tree just shakes its bark,
"Let's just wait till it gets dark!"

Beneath the shade, a dance ensues,
With fireflies twinkling in their shoes.
In the leafy realm, life's a game,
With giggles echoing, never the same.

Songs of the Ringed Trunk

Beneath the shade of stout oak trees,
Beetles bop, swaying with ease.
"My rings are wide, I'm truly grand!"
"Ha! But I'm the tallest in the land!"

A raccoon, quite the funky lad,
Sways to a tune, making all glad.
"Let's start a band," he boldly claimed,
"Just watch out for the squirrels, they're famed!"

"Chop chop, there goes my lovely bark!"
A trunk dons a frown but adds a spark.
"Let's stick together, tall and stout,
In this woodland jam, there's joy about!"

They twirl and spin in laughter bright,
Under the moon's soft silver light.
Each ring a story, each groove a song,
In the heart of nature, they all belong.

Memoirs of the Forest Floor

On the forest floor, chaos reigns,
Where mushrooms poke their curious veins.
"Hey, did you hear about the bee?
He thought he'd win at hide-and-seek!"

A snail replied, with slimy glee,
"Caught in a flower, he lost the spree!"
Next to a log, the toad agreed,
"It's hard to hide with an itch to feed!"

Underneath the twigs and leaves,
Ants chatter 'bout their hidden thieves.
"We've seen it all, from sky to ground,
Life's a treasure hunt, magic unbound!"

The laughter bubbles, bright and warm,
In nature's chaos, there's a charm.
Every creature, big or small,
Adds to the joy—it's a forest ball!

The Tapestry of Tree Rings

In a tree's rings lies history's jest,
"Last winter, I had quite the pest!"
A chipmunk pipes in, full of flair,
"Was it that owl? He gave quite a scare!"

"Let's spin some tales of long ago,
When acorns fell like a golden show!"
The branches sway, a comedic plot,
"Do you remember that knot we all fought?"

"I've seen so many animals sprint,
Especially when a fox leaves a hint!"
The woodpecker nods, "And it's quite prime,
To hear their tales in endless rhyme!"

With each ring, a giggle floats,
As stories grow in cozy notes.
The tapestry's woven with humor grand,
In the woods where laughter meets the land.

Echoing Laughter from the Upper Canopy

Squirrels in suits with a coffee mug,
Telling bad puns, it's quite the hug.
Twigs are snapping, branches sway,
Who knew trees could giggle this way?

A woodpecker's drum beats a silly tune,
Frisky foxes dance 'neath the shimmering moon.
With a bushy tail, the raccoon grins,
Waging a war with acorn skins.

The owls are hooting with belly laughs,
As frogs croak jokes like sloppy drafts.
Leaves rustle softly, adding to the cheer,
Nature's comedians, the audience's dear.

Through branches wide, laughter rings bright,
Echoes of joy under starlit night.
Forest friends cuddle in a comedic clump,
Tickling the trunks, oh, what a jump!

The Language of Branches and Bark

In the language of rustles, whispers take flight,
Branches gossiping in the warm sun light.
A squirrel's chuckle, a chipmunk's joke,
With every swish and sway, they provoke.

A wise old oak feigns a snore,
While the breeze tickles, wanting more.
Barks of laughter escape the shy fawn,
Mirthful meetings greet the dawn.

Caterpillars giggle, in a wiggly race,
While turtles wear expressions, slow on their face.
All creatures in jest, in this leafy retreat,
Join hands and paws in this whimsical feat.

Dancing shadows play on the forest floor,
One tiny acorn starts a loud uproar.
With every chuckle, the woods unite,
In the symphony of laughter, pure delight!

Whispers of the Woodland Giants

Tall trunks towering, secrets they share,
Whispers of wonders float in the air.
The ferns are nodding, the ivy takes note,
Listening closely to the giants who gloat.

A bumblebee buzzes, starting a rhyme,
With a big beetle beatboxing in time.
Mushrooms are giggling, puffing out spores,
Dropping their jokes from the old forest floors.

Lights through the leaves create shadows of fun,
Chasing each other, under the sun.
Sticks in a tussle, friends take a stand,
Giggles and grumbles all over the land.

Where moss-covered giants joke with the breeze,
And a light-hearted breeze sways the leaves with ease.
Mother Nature chuckles, a wink in her eye,
As laughter and levity float up to the sky.

Shadows Beneath the Canopy

Shadows dancing, a playful ballet,
Critters crawl under the branches that sway.
A lizard slips on a leaf, what a fall,
While a toad croaks loudly, "Not my fault at all!"

The breeze tickles whispers, secrets unfold,
As the shadows giggle, their stories retold.
Charming raccoons with a clever chime,
Make fun of the sun, causing laughter to climb.

Underneath boughs, their antics ensue,
Each raucous laugh is a woodsy debut.
On mushroom-made stools, they gather for glee,
Hooting and howling, as silly as can be.

In the twilight glow, they leap and they bound,
Creating a ruckus, a merry old sound.
With friendship and jests, the night grows so bright,
In shadows beneath the canopy, pure delight.

Fables of the Twisted Limbs

In the tree where squirrels prank,
A wise old owl thinks, "Good flank!"
The gossip flows through all the leaves,
As crickets dance in evening eves.

A raccoon dons a pirate hat,
Yelling, "I need a treasure map!"
The branches creak as laughter swells,
And echoes fill the forest dwells.

Beneath the bark, the beetles joke,
While golden sunbeams make them woke.
"I'm the king of this great mound!"
Said one, and laughter spins around.

With every gust, the leaves would giggle,
As playful winds would twist and wiggle.
The jokes of ages softly weave,
Among the limbs, they trick and cleave.

Lifetimes of the Whispering Pines

The pines hold secrets of old quips,
Where even squirrels roll their lips.
One whispers tales of past mishaps,
When owls would fall for their own traps.

A crow once thought he'd take a flight,
But landed flat, what a sight!
He cawed aloud, "I meant to land!"
As chuckles spread across the land.

The acorns hold a family feud,
With each nut squabbling, feeling rude.
"I'm bigger! No, I'm rounder still!"
The laughter echoes on the hill.

Old roots remember the days gone by,
The cat with dreams to touch the sky.
She leapt too high, but oh! The grace,
Now her tales bring smiles to the place.

The Ballet of Branch and Breeze

The branches sway in twisted dance,
While leaves spin down, a funny chance.
They whirl and twirl in sunny light,
As shadows play and give a fright.

The breeze hums tunes, a merry song,
It shakes the limbs and sings along.
A frog jumps in—a muddy splash,
In perfect sync, they share a bash.

Amongst the blooms, a bee does waltz,
But stumbles hard—oh, what a fault!
He buzzes loud, then takes a bow,
Join us, dear friends, here and now!

Oh! A butterfly in ballet shoes,
Steps on a twig, and sings the blues.
Yet giggles rise and fill the space,
In this grand dance, we find our place.

Roots of Resilience

Deep in the soil, old roots unwind,
With jokes and laughter, sweetly timed.
"Why did the twig refuse to bend?"
"To stay away from the tree's bad end!"

The gnarled knots tell tales of cheer,
Of storms they've faced through every year.
"When the wind blows, we hold on tight,"
With smiles that shine into the night.

The burrowing bugs throw a grand feast,
With crunchy leaves being the least.
"Why do the roots enjoy the rain?"
"To wash away all of our pain!"

While raindrops fall with funny plops,
They dance beneath the leafy tops.
So cheers to roots that stand and sprout,
In moments of laughter, we scream and shout!

Nature's Narrative in the Treetop Realm

A squirrel in a hat, quite a sight,
He danced with the breeze, oh, what a flight!
The leaves chuckled low, in whispers they spoke,
As branches twirled and the acorns awoke.

Bright birds in a choir, singing quite bold,
Joked with the breeze, tales of mischief told.
Down below, a fox, with a smirk on his face,
Joined in the laughter, enjoying the chase.

The Elders of the Evergreen

Old trees with wise grins, roots deep in the ground,
Share sagas of nuts and of mischief profound.
The owls crack a joke, in the still of the night,
While raccoons in tuxedos prepare for the fright.

A woodpecker's tap keeps the rhythm alive,
As critters all gather, ready to thrive.
With a wink and a nod, they revel they might,
These elders ensure that the fun is in sight.

A Symphony of Branches

The branches compose a whimsical song,
With rustles and giggles, they all sing along.
The wind plays conductor, a fun little twist,
While roots join the beat, no one can resist.

With each playful rustle, a story unfolds,
Of acorns that tumbled and young trees that told.
A harmony of mischief, high above the ground,
In this merry forest, such joy can be found.

Journey Through Dappled Light

In patches of sun, the shadows dance bright,
With giggles of sunlight that playfully bite.
The mushrooms in grass wear hats of delight,
As frogs leap and croak, what a sight, what a sight!

The butterflies flutter, with grace they float by,
Trading jokes with the bees, oh, me oh my!
Around every corner, life's humor does bloom,
In this joyful forest, there's never a gloom.

Conversations Among the Canopies

Squirrels chatter high and low,
About acorns they will throw.
Birds debate the best flight tricks,
As branches sway and make us laugh with kicks.

A wise old owl gives advice so grand,
While a raccoon tries to lend a hand.
The leaves gossip, rustling in the breeze,
Sharing secrets with the buzzing bees.

A chipmunk shares his newest snack,
As all around, the saplings crack.
Chirps and squawks fill the endless air,
In this canopy of fun, without a care.

Laughter bubbles, with no time to waste,
Every shadow has a smile placed.
Together they dance in the dappled light,
From morning's glow to the fall of night.

The Heartbeat of Root and Leaf

Beneath the bark, a party thrives,
Where tiny creatures spin their jives.
Roots tap dance in the soil below,
While leaves sway gently, putting on a show.

A worm hums tunes of long-lost days,
As fungi join in, adding their praise.
Underneath the leafy crown,
Laughter bubbles, never a frown.

In the shadows, stories swirl around,
Of critters' antics and seeds that abound.
Saplings shout with glee and cheer,
Swaying to a rhythm only they hear.

Tree trunks chuckle at silly tales,
As squirrels juggle their nutty trails.
Life vibrates with a joyous beat,
In the harmony of growth beneath our feet.

Knowledge Embedded in Timber

From rings of wood, wisdom spills,
Each layer echoes the joy-filled thrills.
Crows convene to learn and play,
While bark dressed in green holds tales at bay.

The ancient oaks and pines alike,
Share secrets of seasons, of storms they strike.
A beaver brings a splash of cheer,
Telling logs of plans to engineer.

The whispers of leaves impart a lore,
While deer giggle, asking for more.
What fun it is to stretch and grow,
Under the gaze of the sun's warm glow!

Old roots twirl in a merry dance,
As nature grants each bloom a chance.
In every knot, a story hides,
Liveliness framed in timber's sides.

The Hidden Lives of Treetop Spirits

In the treetops, sprites take flight,
Bouncing on beams of shimmering light.
They weave through branches, giggling loud,
Hiding from the passing cloud.

With acorn hats and leafy cloaks,
They whisper riddles and tell funny jokes.
Each gust of wind brings bursts of cheer,
As they play hide and seek, never in fear.

A tiny fairy tickles a crow,
While a gnome teaches squirrels how to flow.
Dance and flutter amongst the leaves,
Their laughter echoes, oh what a breeze!

As dusk approaches, the stories set sail,
On shafts of twilight, wild they prevail.
In the canopy, fun never ends,
With spirits and friends that nature sends.

Chronicles of the Stalwart Spruces

In a wood where the spruces stood so proud,
A squirrel wore sneakers and danced like a crowd.
He twirled on a branch, causing quite the stare,
As birds cheered him on, what a sight in the air!

A pine with a grin played jokes with the breeze,
Tickling the leaves, making them quiver with ease.
"Why did the tree fall?" it laughed with delight,
"Because it lost its roots in a comedy night!"

Acorns rolled down like a misfit parade,
Chasing their dreams while the forest just swayed.
The moss giggled softly, with a touch of a sigh,
"We're nuts for this tree-party, oh me, oh my!"

The spruces stood tall, with laughter in their bark,
While the sun played hide and seek, sparking a spark.
In this woodland so funny, forever they'll be,
A comedy show high up in the green spree!

Legends of the Verdant Heights

Among the leaves where the wild things pose,
A rabbit told tales, and they tickled his toes.
With hat and a cane, he pranced through the glen,
"Who needs a wizard, when I've got my den?"

The owls hooted softly, with spectacles on,
They pondered the mysteries of dawn and of dawn.
"What's better than wisdom?" they cooed with a grin,
"Why, knowing your buddy is ready to spin!"

The bushes all quivered with gossip galore,
A hedgehog lost socks outside in the floor.
The ferns whispered softly, "It's quite a debacle,
He's always forgetting to dress for a baffle!"

When night fell in whispers, the moon sent a wink,
As creatures gathered 'round for a chuckle and drink.
In the legends of laughter, no shadows reside,
In the verdant heights, joy is the guide!

The Canopy's Keep

Up high in the branches, the parrots all squawked,
They swapped silly stories while the chipmunks just stalked.
"Did you hear about Larry, the sloth who could skate?"
"He zipped through the branches, must have been fate!"

The squirrels sat knitting with twigs and with beads,
Creating odd garments with winks and with needs.
"Here's a vest for a frog!" one chirped with great glee,
"Though he'll need a raincoat for our next jamboree!"

The canopy echoed with laughter and fun,
As critters played tag under warm, golden sun.
A raccoon in a bowtie declared it a race,
But the turtles just chuckled and stayed in their pace!

As dusk cast its charm, the stars took a peek,
The creatures all gathered, their voices unique.
In the keep of the canopy, life's never a bore,
For fun grows like branches, forever and more!

Fables from the Forest's Heart

In a glade where the laughter rang louder than bells,
A fox with a flute played enchanting sweet spells.
He'd charm all the critters, both big and both small,
And each furry friend would dance and enthrall!

The beavers were busy, crafting jokes from their wood,
While the mushrooms just chuckled, feeling quite good.
"Why do we gather?" an old stump raised the query,
"For comical times and to lighten our merry!"

The owls spun around, making wisecrack delights,
As shadows grew longer and filled up the nights.
"Watch out for that twig!", one twitted and squealed,
"Or you'll trip on a laugh—it's surely revealed!"

The heart of the forest was vibrant and bright,
With tales of the quirky amusing the night.
In fables of laughter, the spirits did soar,
For joy in the woodland is found at its core!

Stories in the Sap

In a sticky spot, the squirrels play,
While bees buzz round, they jest and sway.
A wise old owl, with spectacles worn,
Claims he's seen a tree that's better adorned.

The trees all chuckle, roots intertwine,
As critters debate the best tree line.
A raccoon, cheeky, tells a tall tale,
Of golden acorns that dance like a gale.

Frogs join the fray, with leaps in delight,
Giggling past mushrooms, oh what a sight!
With splashes and croaks, they plot a great scheme,
To turn the moonlight into a cream.

As night wraps the woods in a blanket of fun,
Every leaf whispers where laughter has run.
In the whims of the branches, joy has no gap,
Life flows like honey, sweet stories in sap.

Whims of the Wind-Worn Brambles

The brambles twist, in a playful game,
As the breeze whispers secrets, never the same.
A chatter of thorns, they dance in a line,
Riddles of rustle, oh how they entwine!

Bouncing along, a hare takes a leap,
While cherries behind just giggle and peep.
A turtle in shades, with a shell so grand,
Hums a tune while the branches stand.

"Watch out!" cries a dove, "the thorns might bite!"
But laughter erupts, as they gather for night.
With fireflies twinkling like stars in the dark,
The whimsy of nature ignites a bright spark.

In the heart of the brambles, laughter takes flight,
As shadows grow long, they bloom with delight.
Where whispers and giggles combine in the air,
The wind-worn brambles hum traditions so rare.

The Gathering of Woodland Spirits

In the glade under oaks, spirits convene,
With acorns as cups, they toast to the scene.
A fox tells a joke, while the badgers all chime,
Encouraging laughter, oh what a good time!

The ferns have a dance, flapping leaves in a twirl,
While mushrooms applaud, with their caps all a-girl.
They clap and they cheer, it's quite the affair,
With shadows and moonlight, shimmering in air.

An elf with a flute plays a jig so spry,
And butterflies flutter, all dancing nearby.
Each spirit, so merry, losing all sense,
As fireflies join in, lighting up their suspense.

In the heart of the forest, where laughter runs free,
Woodland spirits gather, oh what glee!
Stories unfurl, their laughter divine,
In this playful haven, their hearts intertwine.

Vestiges of the Weathered Trunks

Bark with a story, each wrinkle and line,
Weathered and wise, in laughter they shine.
Branches that sway with a grin and a creak,
Whispering tales, oh so unique.

Old stumps hold councils of critters and kin,
Where tales are spun, and goofy grins begin.
A beetle in boots, with a tambourine,
Taps out a rhythm, a scene to be seen.

Leaves rustle softly, they can't hold their glee,
As winds carry giggles from high to the tree.
Each gust brings a snippet of history told,
In the embrace of the ages, both funny and bold.

From saplings to elders, they revel in cheer,
With knotted wood stories that charm every ear.
A rooty-old party, that all are invited,
In the vestiges laughing, no soul is blighted.

Murmurs in the Misty Grove

In the grove, where shadows play,
Squirrels gossip all day.
They chatter about a lost acorn,
Chewing tales of woe, forlorn.

A raccoon slides down with flair,
Wearing leaves like a tousled heir.
He trips but lands with style,
The grove erupts in laughter, all the while.

Owls hoot in a clumsy rhythm,
Arguing about tree-top wisdom.
Their feathers ruffle, quite a sight,
As branches sway in feathery delight.

The breeze whispers secrets so sweet,
As insects tap dance on tiny feet.
A dance-off breaks, they spin around,
Joyful chaos in the misty ground.

Fables of the Forest Elders

Once the wise old turtle spoke,
"I once tried the vine, but it broke!"
The deer chuckled in gentle jest,
"Did you run, or just take a rest?"

A fox, with charm and a great flair,
Said, "I've got secrets, if you dare!"
The owls rolled eyes, not impressed,
"Your pranks have us all quite distressed!"

The porcupine, with quills held high,
Claimed he could dance and even fly.
The laughter echoed through the trees,
"Go ahead, but mind the bees!"

In this forest, tales intertwine,
Each creature's jest, a twist of divine.
With every smile, and every cheer,
The fables grow, year after year.

The Watchful Eyes of Nature

Tiny critters peek from their lair,
With mischief brewing in the air.
A chubby hedgehog rolls by fast,
"Did you see that? I'm quite the blast!"

The rabbits gossip in a flurry,
"Did you hear about that squirrel's worry?
He forgot where he stashed his prize,
Now he just pouts and sighs."

The wise old badger shakes his head,
"Kids these days," he softly said.
"Once I lost a shoe in a race,
But I found it in the silliest place!"

Nature's laughter is a tune,
Celebrated under the light of the moon.
With every glance, a chuckle grows,
In the woods where the mischief flows.

Serenade of the Sunlit Glens

In sunny glens where dances unfold,
Grasshoppers strut, incredibly bold.
One slipped and tumbled head over heels,
Outrageous giggles as laughter steals.

The daisies sway and join the song,
"Let's play follow the bee along!"
A ladybug boasts of her shiny shell,
While ants march in a tidy hotel.

A parrot flutters, copycat charm,
"Mimic me quick, it's a world of warm!"
But when he sneezes, the humor blares,
As feathers scatter, unaware of stares.

In these glens where sunshine streams,
All creatures weave whimsical dreams.
Each chirp and chuckle, pure delight,
A serenade of joy, in the highlight.

Mar tales of the Wind's Embrace

Up high the whispers twirl and dance,
A squirrel dons a hat, thinks it's a chance.
Branches shake with laughter, oh what a sight,
While the breeze takes a swing, oh what a flight!

The leaves trade gossip, secrets they share,
A shy little frog jumps up without care.
"Did you hear the owl stutter, late last night?"
"Only when the fireflies started a light!"

A raccoon plays tricks with acorn-filled pies,
"Best held for dessert!" he shouts with surprise.
The wind gives a chuckle, rolling along,
Spreading the joy in a whimsical song.

And so in the canopy, mischief runs free,
With giggles and gaffes, the tallest of trees.
A carnival hidden, it winks with glee,
In a world where the laughter is light as can be.

Sentinels of the Sunlit Sky

In the branches, the parakeets wear shades,
Chirping gossip that never fades.
"Did you see that cloud with a funny face?"
It floated by, oh what a grace!

The owls juggle acorns, all night they play,
"Who needs to sleep, let's dance the day!"
Bees paint the blossoms in bright, silly hues,
While the sun makes a joke about weather clues.

The sunlight tickles, the shadows giggle,
As turtles wear hats and squirrels wiggle.
"Come join the hoedown," the branches decree,
A party erupts in the sunlit spree!

So here in the heights where the laughter is grand,
The creatures unite, a merry band.
With sunshine as their stage, fun never dies,
As the sentinels watch from the blue, bright skies.

The Enchanted Understory

Beneath leafy umbrellas, the party begins,
Where mushrooms wear shoes and dance with grins.
The bugs hold a concert, a zesty delight,
While ants tap their feet, keeping rhythm so tight.

A hedgehog tells stories, humorous spins,
"Last week I was chased by a pack of chins!"
The beetles all chuckle, rolling in mirth,
As they celebrate life, and their little earth.

The ferns twist and twirl in a leafy ballet,
With roots that are gossiping all through the day.
"Did you hear the tale of that butterfly's fling?"
"Oh darling, it's funny, let's dance and sing!"

In this hidden realm where the giggles abound,
The wonders of nature are cheerful and sound.
To be lost in the laughter, the forests conspire,
Enchanted and joyful, they lift hearts higher.

Laments of Lush Verduro

In the thicket, the thyme makes a terrible mess,
While the daisies compete for the title of best dress.
"I'm the fanciest flower here, can't you tell?"
The dandelions giggle, "Oh, we know you well!"

A raccoon's mournful song echoes through the trees,
"Why can't I find food that's more than just cheese?"
The elderflower laughs, fluttering in breeze,
"A banquet awaits, we'll feast if you please!"

The willow weeps over a lost wooden shoe,
While the ferns spill their ink, making poems new.
"Write about potlucks, and parties divine,"
The buttercups shout, "Let's drink some sweet wine!"

Amidst the lush greens, life's quirkiness blooms,
With chuckles and sighs filling up the rooms.
Even laments can turn bright and not dreary,
In the laughter of foliage, we find it cheery!

www.ingramcontent.com/pod-product-compliance
Lightning Source LLC
Chambersburg PA
CBHW071824160426
43209CB00003B/205